If & When We Wake

Poems by Francis Daulerio

Artwork by Scott Hutchison

Attention schools and businesses: for discounted copies on large
orders, please contact the publisher directly.

For information contact:
Unsolicited Press
Portland, Oregon
www.unsolicitedpress.com
orders@unsolicitedpress.com
619-354-8005

Cover Image: Scott Hutchison.
Cover Designer: Savannah Stewart

ISBN-13: 978-0692604175

For my grandfather

Contents

III

Preface

It's a warm Saturday afternoon in southeastern Pennsylvania, and I've returned to the home where my grandparents lived to do some carpentry work and cleaning and remember the younger part of my life I spent in this place. My grandmother is sick, and this house will have to sell to help pay for the time she has left, so our small family has been flocking back in waves to tend to odds and ends, reminiscing more than working, really.

I'm sitting on the ground, the furniture gone, watching the first day of September blow bits of fresh sawdust across the pavers that replaced the cracked concrete slab. I need a beer, but the refrigerator was hauled out last week. The echo of my grandfather's pellet gun is long gone, too, but the neighbor is putting a new roof on his shed, and the pop of his framing nailer is close enough to take me to the memories I'm hunting, the childhood that lives and dies within the pages of this book.

It's been eleven years since my grandfather passed, three years since Scott and I first sent this book off to print, and only three months since his devastating suicide. Things are different now. Louder in a lot of ways. Quieter in others. The overwhelming excitement of moving on to a new project together is gone, swapped out for what feels like a brick in my gut and a new type of longing I hadn't yet experienced. My granddad's garden is gone, too, dug up some years ago and sodded over, and without the map of this place that I keep inside myself, you'd never even know it had been here. This is something I try to remind myself of when I start to feel the panic of inadequacy seeping in or catch myself searching for purpose in life. We're here for awhile. Then we're not. It's that simple.

When I started writing the poems that eventually became this book, I didn't quite know what I was trying to accomplish. I'd been carrying around a sadness for years, and unsure of how to shake it, I turned to poetry as an outlet, talking out ideas into my phone recorder during long, dark morning drives down the Pennsylvania Turnpike. Each day, a new flash of memory would fall out of the ether, and the deeper I dug into myself, the more fragments of life I found. Scott called them meditations. Snippets. Mostly about this place and the people who lived here. Images of my youth made strange when reexamined from a more adult perspective. It was this act of forcibly remembering that helped me drag myself across that great expanse of grief and into some sort of understanding about all of this. Not happiness, exactly. Something more essential.

If & When We Wake is an attempt at authenticity. It's a reminder that we are going to die, and a call to use our inevitable mortality as fuel to help propel us into something remarkable before we sputter out. While writing, I'd imagined it could function as a declaration of life in spite of death, though maybe it ended up being less ferocious than I'd wanted. Looking back on the collection now in the wake of Scott's passing, I fear these poems may have focused too much on the darkness, but I hope you'll see the light in them. I hope they'll serve as a reminder that, as cold and empty as life can get, there exists in all of us the potential for growth and happiness and beauty, and although that potential changes as our lives evolve, it never goes away. It's as alive as we are. I wish I'd gone hunting for these words sooner, before my grandfather's medical setbacks and life changes pushed him to shut down and will the collapse to come faster than it needed to. I wish I could have found them for Scott, too, when his world became too bleak and the dark cavern of depression finally caved in on him. I miss them both in ways I can't talk about. I miss the different people I was when I knew them. And I'm learning, as each day passes, I miss the one that came before it more and more. Still, I believe in the future. If we keep our eyes ever forward, there's a hope that things can get better.

I'll probably never sit in this spot again, so I'm going to close my eyes and remember it as I want to: I'm small. My mop of black hair is combed to the side and full of sweat. I'm sitting on this patio in a lawn chair next to my grandfather, who's wearing an unbuttoned plaid shirt, a WWII vet hat, and drinking a Yuengling Light, eyes fixed on the corner of his small garden, waiting for the mouse he's been tracking to surface between the tomato cages. There's poison in this garden, too, but I'm not supposed to tell anyone. The sun is shining, and far across the sea Scott is young, too, shy like me, and quiet. We all have so much time left, even the mouse, who dodges the incoming pellet and darts back into the brush unharmed. We don't yet know the weight of panic, and we're all the lighter for it. Our futures are wide open and so full of magic.
We can do anything.
There's not a cloud in the sky.

Francis
September 1, 2018
Lafayette Hill, Pennsylvania

Let us cultivate our garden

-Voltaire

If & When We Wake

Only in the quietest moments
do we see
the reviving sun
and taste the dew
on bending blades of grass.

We rise with shouts
against the darkness
and claw our way
toward daylight.

I

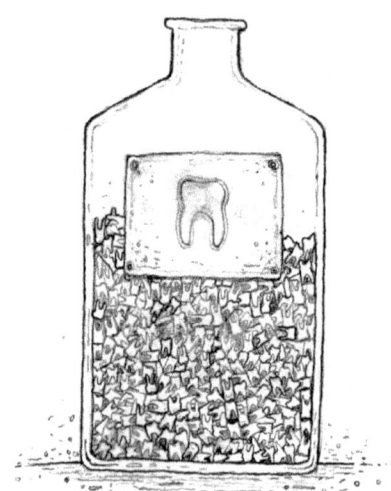

Kept Out of Reach

I have a childhood
somewhere inside me,
stashed away like baby teeth
in a medicine bottle.

Now I'm old enough to open
it, so I open it
and peer into the white.

Hunter

Sunday nights were yellow-lamped
dinners—
        a squeaky table,
        quiet conversation
        over pheasant soup,
        and tap water
        in depression glass tumblers.

My grandfather caught
what we ate
until he was too old
to trudge through
the early dawn
and steady his eye
down the cold barrel.

Meditations on Vegetable Gardens

I.
I remember watching you
thumb rat poison into
cherry tomatoes,
hiding them between the dark moss
of the rail ties
surrounding your humility
garden.

I want to breathe in the dirt—
      I want to remember
            your shoes.

II.
I was knee-high and sun burnt,
learning how to plant leeks
and trim dead blooms.

You crushed a mouse beneath your foot;
its small bones resonated from the concrete patio
as I scanned the dirt for seedlings.

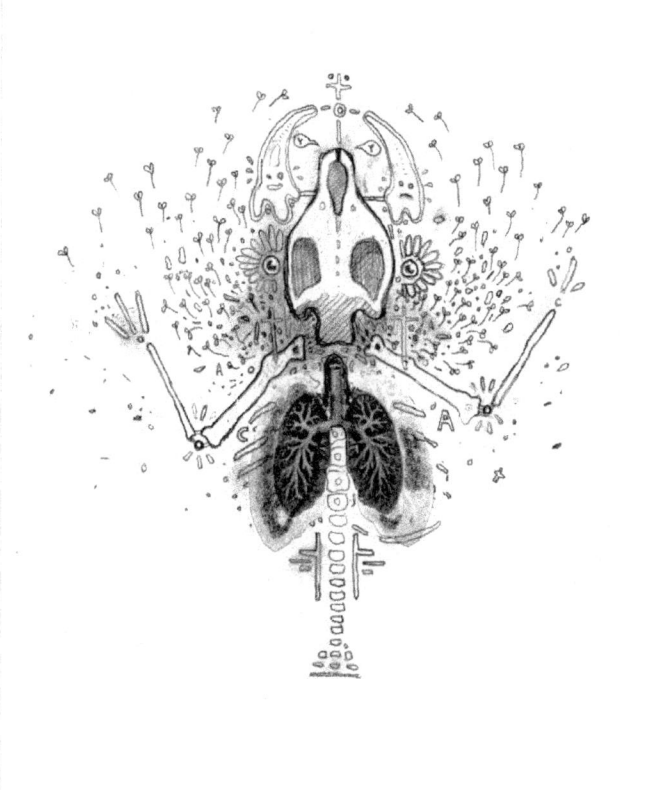

III.
I liked my perception when I was young.
Grass could whisper,
trees got stoned on sunlight,
and people never left for good.

Now I dip pot in embalming fluid
and scatter salt like ashes
in your vegetable garden.

Knowledge is such shit.

Hospice

I stared at the hospital bed
in your living room
as I imagine they stared
at the Space Needle
in 1962.

It should have been torn down—
It was given the chance
to reach its unnatural hands
too close to Heaven.

Toward Those Bright Lights

You planned your escape
for February fifth.
You didn't tell anyone,
but in the days preceding
you started shifting in your sleep
to loosen the muscle
and stretch the skin.

It must have been uncomfortable,
but you never let on.
You just lay in your bed,
blue eyes upward,
looking for a way
through.

When my father's father died
he dreamt of phone calls.
I'm here, Frank. Go back to sleep.
Instead, you kept it tight-lipped—

You dragged a pine branch behind you
to scratch out your tracks
on your way
up.

In Hibernation

Sparrows trip
through the hemlock—

what can we do
when winter is sleeping
and the juniper berries have dried?

As Far As I Know

I remember things
in flashes,
       inaccurately.

The smell of smashed walnuts
in the Wissahickon valley
and the sound tires made
popping over gravel.

The water
rushing over rocks
as fast as we aged,

and the way my face reflected
your face
in rain-soaked leaves.

The clatter of hammers on nails on fence posts
and the weight of everything
kept in.

How did I get here?

Were you there with me then?

Something will always be
a bit off
like crooked Windsor knots
at quickly planned funerals.

Seconds Before the Blast

When I called to tell her
you were gone,
I pictured her face
as she picked up the phone.

I imagined her smiling—
a barefoot girl
chasing her shadow
on a clear, Hiroshima day.

Gatherer

Ten years later—
still catching myself
feeling around with my tongue
for buckshot
in my dinner.

Personification

This house is different
without you.
I'll lie and say I like it
better.

I'm hearing new voices.
Dripping faucets,
bare feet on hardwood—

We're scared of the silence

and so the shingles whisper
and the door hinges squeal
and the teapot seems to whistle
a bit louder.

I   like   it   better.

Cognitive Dissonance; or, Following a Death

Sometimes when I venture
into the basement to borrow a hammer
I swear to God
I hear you put your glasses down
on the table
and walk away.

Reincarnation

I've taken to writing poems
on small, wrinkled papers
and dropping them from my bedroom window
to dance with the drifting snow
and take root in my vegetable garden.

In the spring they will sprout
and blossom with grape tomatoes
and fresh basil
and grow into something I could never
create alone.

On a Clear Day

When the leaves give way
to the sky
I pretend
if I squint just a little tighter
I'll be able to see
backwards.

Sometimes I almost can, too.

I keep catching myself talking to passed relatives
when I'm supposed to be talking to God

It feels like I'm
in the woods,
looking for guidance—
stars that collapsed
before I was born
are only now
touching me
with their light.

Across the Synaptic Gap

I needed to hear
myself,
so I sat with memory
and listened.

I whispered songs
you taught me—
     little hymns
          my muscles remembered.

I fell out of myself
so you could fall
back into me.

I did this in remembrance,
and forgot myself
in my remembering.

Self-Help

> Crisp leaves
> singing through cattails
> thriving in the muck—
> > a dilating sunlight.
>
> I am going to find beauty in your absence
> if it fucking kills me.

II

Ground Rules

There will be no talk
of politics
or organized religion,
no talk of wars or weapons
or medicines and funding
or the budget
or the deficit
or the fleeting idea of The Dream.

There will be no discussion
of parties
or agendas
or the past
or the future
or FOREVER AND EVER [amen].

There will be no thought
of cancer
or aneurisms bursting,
no thought of functions ceasing
or the decreasing will to live.

There will be no I.
There will be no you.
There will be no us.
There will be no them—

There will only be
        The leaves falling softly
                into the creek bed
            and the knowing
                    that we are only here
                right
                        now.

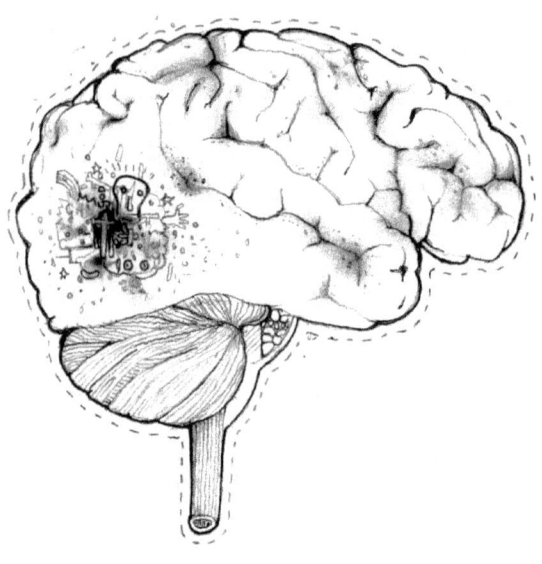

Cracking Back Through

Fast forward
through the thaw—

We sprout
from our homes,
muddy boots,
almost warm
if not for the wind.

Let existence explode,
pump life back into itself,
and
grow.

On Second Chances

Little tributaries
guide my feet
to a river
I used to wade through.

Now it just covers
my ankles—

I still taste
the mouthful of inkberries
and the ipecac
that brought me back
to life.

.

Spring Hymn

I.
When the world came back
to life
I had to remind myself
that it was not
the same.

The blooms were
smaller;
some were new,
some had split
and branched off
toward opposite sides of Heaven.

Some had not returned at all,
and I noticed their absence.

II.
And if we had the resilience
of spring blossoms
on wind-torn limbs,
we would glow
our pinks and whites
       temporarily
       against graying bark,

as stars
blast light
into darkness.

III.
In the chirping mornings of May
an old wind crosses
from the eastern corner of the lake
bringing the chill
of late October—

       as warm and promising
       as new life is,
       there is an end
       that laps closer to our banks
       with each waking.

A Ghost Story

A 5:15 alarm pulls me back
into the world—
    spearmint bathroom,
    quiet kitchen.

I float into the purple
dew-wet morning,
taking no notice
of the peaking lilies
or the fading
little sliver of the moon.

Annuals

In the backyard
there are small lumps
where I dug up the earth
with my stained hands
to bury what will become
scallions.

The bursts of green
that fed on frost
will pop and bolt
to be plucked in May
and swallowed with their hope
of June.

Like Bibles on Pulpits

Swimming naked
in a June-warmed Tennessee
lake—

Rain falls wild
like the gospel,
and thunder crashes
down
under God's big
watery eye.

June 24th

This morning, the flowers
woke up like a cat stretching
her arms,
claws popping out
            and blooming.

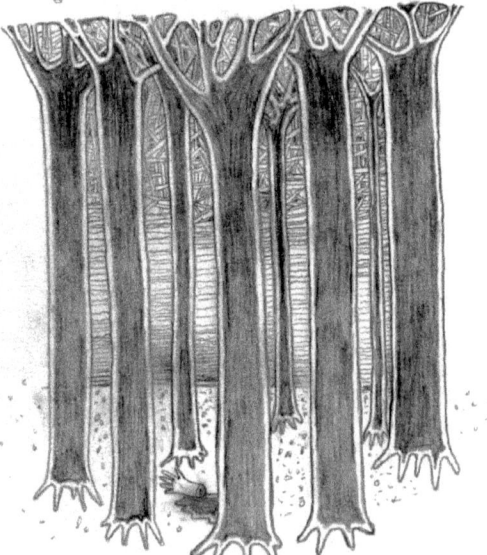

Amendment

There is more to life
than deer tracks
and studying seed schedules
in the Farmer's Almanac.

The underwriters numberfuck
everyone
and God will find us
no matter how deep
we bury ourselves
in the trees.

Seared Spoons; or, A State Line
                              for Justin

> It wasn't suicide, really.
> He was forced to
>   *do it.*
> I told him not to
>   *listen to them,*
> but he didn't hear me.

>   We were in different states.

Iridescence; or, Finding Enlightenment

It's ten o'clock
and the dancing night
bugs bounce
from wall
to dirt
to fence.

A Japanese beetle wakes
on my porch screen
and flies
into the glow
of citronella—

                I think he confused it for Heaven.

Covering Roadways Like Skin Over Vessels

At 5:30 in the morning
we speak to each other,
        the fog and I,
about the emptiness beneath.

We do our best to cover it up
        in one way or another.

Obituary for a Gypsy

In a public bathroom
in a Delaware state park
two moths huddle near a corner
above a sink.

One is dead.

Trapped in a spider web,
it hangs, inanimate—
a powdery specter.

The other pounds its silent lament
against the wall:

    Such a fucked way to go.

Kierkegaard's Thunderstorm

The thoughtless rain washes
dew from my early-morning
window screens.

I wait for the day
when I can simply *do*
as the Earth rains for want of rain.

Early Morning Cat Burglar

I wake up
at three o'clock in the morning
and scribble words
on the corner of a napkin that my cat will later
drag under the bed
and hide in her nest of lost poetry.

Turning three or four times
she settles down
to rest
in my thoughts
and dreams of ghosts
in the garden.

They always say, "God never gives you more
than you can handle"

Sitting on our sagging sofa,
the weather channel on
mute—

my wife and I stare
at opposite walls,
taking turns
exhaling,
and promising
that everything will
work out
for the best.

Beeps & Clicks; or, A Three-Day Recovery

> Two years ago my body started lying to me.
> One year ago I tried to stop it.
> I think I'm making progress;
> the beeps and clicks of emergency room dialogue
> are sounding less familiar, now.

The Great Migration

for Sophie

Until I see
you again,
take care of yourself.

Stay warm,
and check in
if you get the chance.

Don't forget the way
the wind smells,
and keep your nose down.

Know that we're always
thinking of you,

and don't forget
                    to run.

Existentially Speaking

I want to rip my thumbs out at the knuckles
and run wild through damp meadows
of wind-bent grass—

I want it to hurt
because it was meant to.

All's Well That Ends

"Don't ever tell anybody anything. If you do, you start
missing everybody"

-J.D. Salinger

Who needs poetry
anyway?

There're enough stars
in that giant, blurry sky
as it is.

Who needs a new light?

Nobody
needs to go out
finding *new light*.

With Calloused Feet To Carry Us

On Tuesday morning I will burn
my social security card,
walk out of work,
and throw my
fucking key fob
into the toilet.

I'll call your mom
to see if you can come out and play
and we'll hop the fence
and be late for dinner.

On Traveling Abroad

Day 1: Transatlantic Transfers

Sitting in an airport terminal
a graying couple settles
behind me
with locked fingers
and brittle
conversation.

There are fading chairs
and tattered carpets
and I am bound
for Scotland
reading Kerouac
and my wife is home
waiting

for the red to blush through
our tomato plants
on this tiny day in a giant
July.

Day 2: Walking Along the North Sea

Coal burning
through chimney pots,
spitting dust over the sea—

the taste is romantic,
like faith (now)
or tourism.

Day 5: The Pieces I Can Carry

A loose strand of hair
doesn't have a smell.
It doesn't have a taste
or a memory
or a set of eyes to gaze back at me
and speak.

I found a strand of her hair
in my suitcase
next to some postcards
and a universal adapter.

It really isn't her,
but I wrap it around my finger
like twine
as if I'd otherwise forget.

BURD

Day 8: Homesick; or, Ionesco's Travel Diary

I'm sitting in a Scottish park
on a Scottish bench
drinking a bottle of Scottish water
listening to the Scottish birds chirping
in their Scottish brogues
and rolling their Scottish syllables.

A Scottish lawnmower passes behind me
and the exhaust smells like a warm
American backyard day
with German sausages on a Japanese grill.
      I drag it into my lungs
            but the taste is five hours
            off.

Return

> To a gentle home
> with water crawling
> over downed branches
> and nuthatches whispering
> through forsythia—
>> not to disturb the quiet
>> but to discourage the noise.

III

For My Wife

There are bright afternoons
when I watch her snipping thyme
from the windowsill,
quietly singing to herself

and in those moments
I'm certain
that if she cracked me open
I'd emit light.

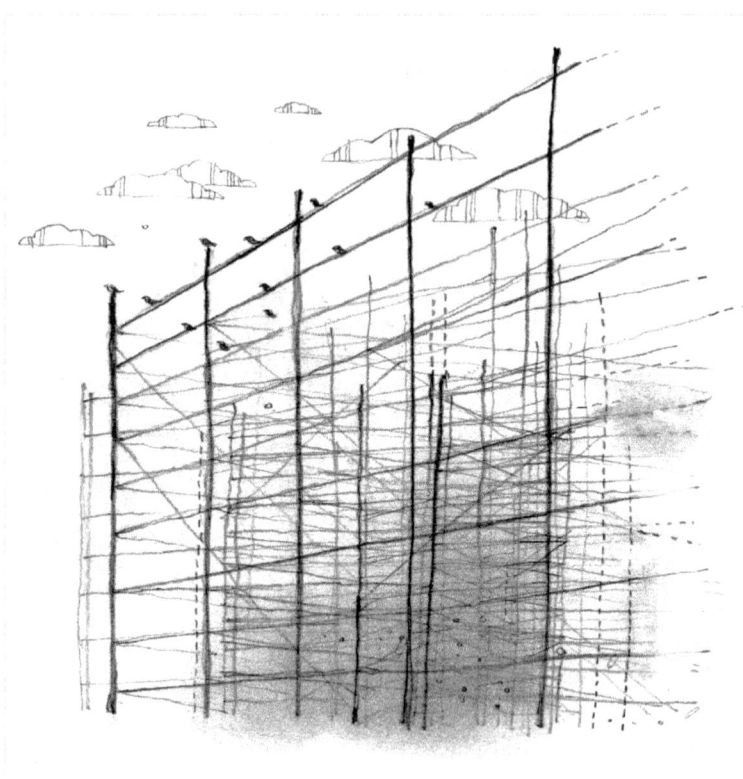

August 30th

It's a humid evening
and the robins are whistling
like construction workers
in their scaffolding.

We walk a little slower,
let them take us in.

Leah tells me not to stare:
it only encourages them.

Summer Hymn

My wife
is patches of farmland
pushed into the
Pennsylvania countryside.

I peel the zinnia petals
from my back.

Perennials Grow Beneath Us

There is a maple in her mother's backyard
with sap
and nests
and dirt
and hope
and our names carved deep into the green
skin.

We grow with the branches,
and I will love her
even when spring lilies sprout
from under its fallen trunk.

Beckoning; or, From a Mail Slot

> Her letters—
> like children sticking out
> their tongues in hopes
> of a chase.

When the Morning Wakes Us

Her eyes make
what was once flat
not flat
and what felt
like a shuttered window
feel like an open door.

Wedding Vows

There are nights when I can't
believe you
love me.
But you do,
because we dance
like imbeciles
and the moon hangs
like God's streetlight
and our one,
        two,
            three,
   one,
      two,
         three
bounces like our laughter
into the night.

Pillow Talk

I'll fall asleep
desperately
in love.

On her cotton sheets
I'll wake up
tired.

There are Comets! There are Earthquakes!
There are Famines! There are Plagues!

Sitting quietly,
bullfrogs chirping
nervously
in the quickly drying creek bed—

I will never know
if things aren't
already as they should
be.

Autumn Hymn

Give us this day
a look into the past
and a quiet place
to sit
and watch
the geese
fall
into formation
overtop the birches.

October 29th; or, Today it Finally Smells Like Fall

Smoke
from neighboring chimneys
hangs over me
like ghosts
longing
to be
sucked back in
through a fresh set
of lungs.

In Filtered Sunlight

I want to believe
our beyond is slow sap
on stiff needles.

I want to seep down
into you
until we are shed
on the forest floor.

November 19th

> The neighboring farm
> is burning
> scrap wood and leaves
> and I could sit here
> all night
> taking
>
>   slow,
>
>   deep
>
>   breaths,
>
> forgetting everything
> I didn't want to
> learn
> this year.

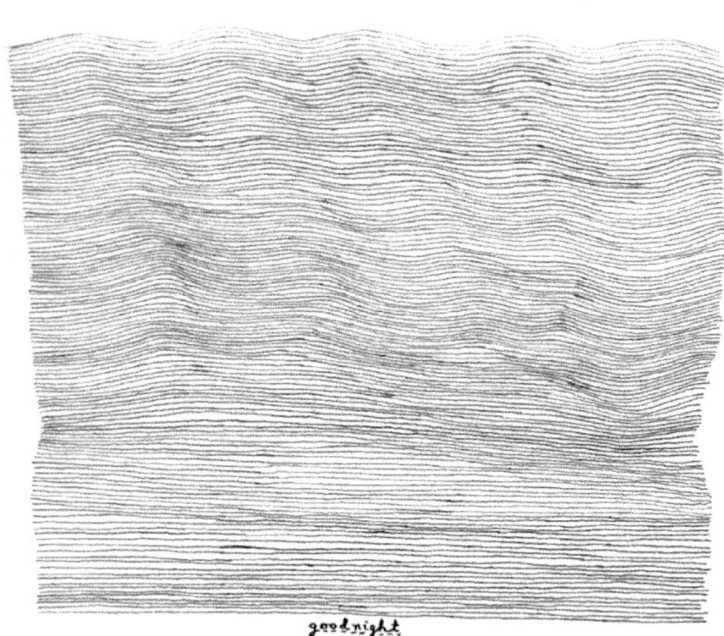

goodnight

Her Body as Oxygen

I will kiss you
goodnight
and we will drift off
to the sounds of the swerving
cars through the now
broken latch.

The tires in the slush
sound like a beach's waves
and I close my eyes,
hold my breath
under a swell of blankets—

the current of your body.

New Year's Resolution

Everything is settling—
the birds into their feather-twig nests,
the sun into its sleep beyond the pines,
the clouds over southeastern Pennsylvania,
the salt crystals into nooks in the asphalt,
and so now I am settling in
with a small glass of neat whiskey,
ready to watch the snow settle
over our worry.

To Age Like Ice

I suppose an icicle grows in reverse
just as we grow
away from ourselves—
dripping
bit by bit
until we simply mix
into the melt.

February 27th

In a bucket
leaking slowly through
the winter,
the deer corn is turning
into whiskey.

The Good Winter: A Hymn

> I trust our hands
> in the purpling hours
> of this good winter.
>
> They build fires
> and fold to grip,
> vessels over vessels,
>
> and we will stay
> warm in this glow
> through and through
> the night.

Post Script

Let us remember to love,
I you
and you me,
and we will rise above ourselves
and Time.

Know us for what we are—
miracles that build fires from timber in winter.

Let us.

Poems in this collection spent their formative years in the following journals:

2River View

A Clean, Well-Lighted Place

Barrow Street

Crack the Spine

Escarp

The Fictioneer

Poetry Quarterly

The Shot Glass Journal

Stone Highway Review

Whiskey Island

Written River

Acknowledgements

I'd like to thank my incredible wife, Leah, for her love and inspiration, my parents for their constant support, my family and friends across the country, Dorian Geisler, Genevieve Betts, Elise Brand, and Malarie Grace for teaching me how to write, Rubie and the UP team, Rich Appel for his encouragement and for editing this mess of poems time after time, and anyone who happens to find themselves holding a copy of this book.

~ Francis

I would like to thank Courtney Brown, my family and Frightened Rabbit.

~ Scott

About the Author

Francis Daulerio is the author of *If & When We Wake* (2015) and *Please Plant This Book* (2018), which benefits the American Foundation for Suicide Prevention. He studied Creative Writing at Arcadia University.

He lives in southeastern Pennsylvania with his wife, children, and a small herd of deer.

More information can be found at www.francisdaulerio.com

About the Artist

Scott Hutchison studied illustration at the Glasgow School of Art.

He is the lead singer and guitarist for the Scottish rock band, Frightened Rabbit.

More information can be found at www.frightenedrabbit.com

*A portion of the proceeds from this book have been donated to
The Scott Hutchison Foundation*